LONDON IN THE THIRTIES

Mike Seaborne

Cyril Arapoff

Cyril Arapoff
LONDON IN THE THIRTIES

Born in Warsaw in 1898, Kyril Semeonovitch Arapov came to England with his mother in 1919 having been forced to leave Russia because of his family's former high-ranking position under the Czar and the Imperialist sympathies of certain members of the family. During the late 1920s and early 1930s Arapoff (as he subsequently spelt his name) spent most of his time in Paris and in Germany where he probably kept himself by tutoring. He was fluent in four languages, having been educated in French-speaking Switzerland and in Italy, where his father was Russian Consul in Florence until his death in 1909. It was not until 1932 or 1933 that Arapoff began to develop an interest in photography, and he then spent a period of six months learning the techniques of the craft at the noted portrait studio of Annelise Kretschmer in Dortmund.

Returning to England late in 1933, Arapoff went to Oxford where his mother had become governess to another Russian emigré family. He established a portrait studio there and was so successful that by 1935 he was considered by many to be the leading portrait photographer in Oxford. As well as studio work, he became involved in theatrical and ballet photography, recording among other things the productions of the Oxford University Dramatic Society and the Markova/Dolin Ballet Company, for which he was the official photographer between 1935 and 1937. His pictures appeared in numerous publications and he even provided the cover illustrations for the first two issues of Richard Buckle's *Ballet* magazine in 1939.

Arapoff also developed a great interest in documentary photography, a genre which, in England, became established in the mid-1930s with the rise of popular picture magazines modelled on the successful German illustrated press of the 1920s. Many of the best photographers of this field were either German or, like Arapoff, had been working in Germany prior to the rise to power of Hitler in 1933 when they chose, or were forced, to leave, some of them coming to England. Much of Arapoff's documentary photography of the 1930s was carried out in London, and it is from this material, which has been acquired by the Museum of London, that the illustrations in this book have been chosen.

Among the subjects featured here are the River Thames, the Caledonian Market, hop-pickers and an East End slum tenement. Many of these photographs were originally used in illustrated magazines, notably the *Geographical Magazine* which published several major stories using Arapoff's pictures. The photographs of Hanbury Buildings, the tenement in Poplar which Arapoff photographed in 1939, were the result of a commission from *Picture Post,* a magazine which he greatly admired, and which was edited by the Hungarian, Stefan Lorant, who also had emigrated from Germany in the early 1930s.

As a photographer, Arapoff quickly achieved a high critical reputation. He exhibited his work regularly throughout the 1930s and received many awards and glowing reviews. R F Hunter Limited, British importers of the German-made Rolleiflex camera which Arapoff used, sponsored a major exhibition of his work in London in 1935, and Jan Gordon, reviewing the exhibition for *The Observer* wrote: '. . . a remarkable series of photographs . . . Arapoff is successful, chiefly because he relies on an almost instinctive sense of apt arrange-

Lighters and sailing barges in the Pool of London

Front cover and title page

A scene at Brentford locks, where the Grand Union Canal joins the River Thames, 1935

ment assisting an acute perception of the 'vital' elements in a scene.' *The Sunday Times* had already described Arapoff's work as marking 'an important stage in the development of British photography'.

In 1937, Arapoff was involved as a 'stills' photographer in the making of a documentary film about Oxford. This was an important experience for him and pointed the way for the future development of his career. In 1939, he undertook stills photography for the Strand Film Company, by whom, in 1941, he was appointed an Assistant Cameraman. As a result, he closed his studio in Oxford and moved to London. In 1942 he joined the official Crown Film Unit and from then on he pursued his career in the documentary film industry, working on a number of important films and distinguishing himself with his camerawork. Between 1952 and 1955, he worked with the distinguished film director, Alberto Cavalcanti, in Brazil, and after a period of freelancing in various parts of the world, he returned to England in 1961 to work for the National Coal Board Film Unit. Arapoff remained there until his death in 1976.

Mike Seaborne, January 1988

Arapoff took many street photographs of children in the East End of London

Left

This photograph was taken in Germany, where Cyril Arapoff studied photography, 1933

A view from the steps of the National Gallery, looking towards
St Martin's Church

A group of boys outside a second-hand shop in the vicinity of Aldgate

Children playing on an artificial 'beach' created on the north
bank of the River near Tower Bridge

A typical working-class street in Poplar

The River near Kew Bridge

Sailing barges and wharfside cranes at Wapping

A family of hop-pickers having their lunch-break. The atmosphere during the three-week picking season resembled that of a holiday camp

Women from London's East End having a 'holiday with pay!'
working in the hop fields of Kent. The tradition of working-class
Londoners going hop-picking goes back at least to the eighteenth
century

The picked hops were collected in a large sack attached beneath
a wooden tripod which held the mouth of the sack open

Enjoying a well-earned short break

A second-hand bookstall. During the 1930s this street market
became a mecca for bargain-hunters and antique collectors

A stall specialising in the sale of dartboards. The market was originally founded in 1855 for the sale of cattle, but by the turn of the century the tradition of a street market being held there every Friday was firmly established

A second-hand carpet stall. Before the Second World War the
Caledonian was the largest and most popular street market in
London

A stall selling spare parts for motor cars and motor cycles. It was said that at one stall it was possible to buy a complete motor car – in parts!

This stall sold ornamental china and bric-a-brac. There were two
classes of stall-holder – the 'cheap-jacks' who sold mostly junk,
and the 'silver kings' whose stalls were spread with glittering dis-
plays of polished silver, much of it of doubtful ownership

This is one of the market's 'characters' whose selling technique involved colourful demonstrations!

This tenement, situated near Poplar High Street, was one of the
worst slums in East London. It had previously been derelict, but
was 'tarted-up' and relet without proper repairs being made, a fact
which the new tenants soon became all too aware of

This small child's brother was killed when the fire-place, which was defective, collapsed

Mr Izaat, the caretaker, *(left)* had an impossible job. He is seen
here inspecting a hole in the gutter of the roof which was causing
the wall of the flat below to become water-logged

Children were denied access to this adjacent empty lot, even
though it served no useful purpose

This ground-floor passageway was flooded by water overflowing from the lavatories upstairs. The drains were blocked, thus preventing the water from flowing away

As though trapped in a prison cell, the children had only a tiny sunken courtyard in which to play

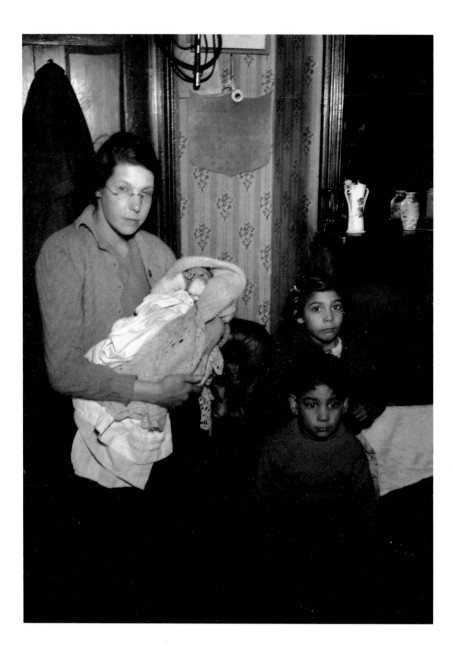

Mrs Mix in her dismal flat with three of her children. The vent for
the outdoor lavatories overlooked her living room, endangering
the children's health

Unable, individually, to persuade the landlord to make urgent
repairs, the tenants formed themselves into a Tenants Association
and decided upon a rent strike to put the landlord under pressure.
Here, a group of women discuss this forthcoming collective action

Mr Mix *(left)* and Mr Roach compare rent books to make sure that
they are fully paid-up prior to the date the rent strike was called.
Any arrears might prejudice their case if it went to court

Mr Mix with one of his small children, uncertain of what the
outcome of the rent strike would be. In the event, the strike lasted
for many weeks until finally the landlord issued summonses
against the tenants, and the case went to court. The judge,
however, found in favour of the tenants and awarded them a stay
of all rent due and for the next eighteen months

The pictures in this booklet are from the Museum of London Collection. The photographs are reproduced by kind permission of the Trustees of the Imperial War Museum. They have been reproduced from the photographers' original prints.

The publisher would like to thank: Mike Seaborne, Curator of the Museum's Historic Photographs Collection for compiling this booklet; the Museum of London for allowing me access to the Collection; and all the other people who have assisted in the production.

Dirk Nishen will be pleased to send you further information about the Photo Library and a copy of his current catalogue

Set in Berthold Poppl Pontifex regular
Phototypesetting   Nagel Fototype, D-Berlin
Origination   ORT Kirchner + Graser, D-Berlin
Printing   H Heenemann, D-Berlin
Binding   H Hensch, D-Berlin
Printed in Germany

ISBN 1 85378 106 1

Dirk Nishen Publishing
19 Doughty Street   London
WC1N 2PT   Great Britain
01 242 0185

NiSHEN
PHOTOGRAPHY